# Grieg

## PIANO CONCERTO IN A MINOR OP.16
## SOLO PIANO ARRANGEMENT

# Edvard Hagerup Grieg

(1843 ~ 1907)

# *INDEX*

# Piano Concerto in A minor

## Solo piano arrangement

Arranged and Edited by
Isaac CHOI and Eun-han LEE

## I

8

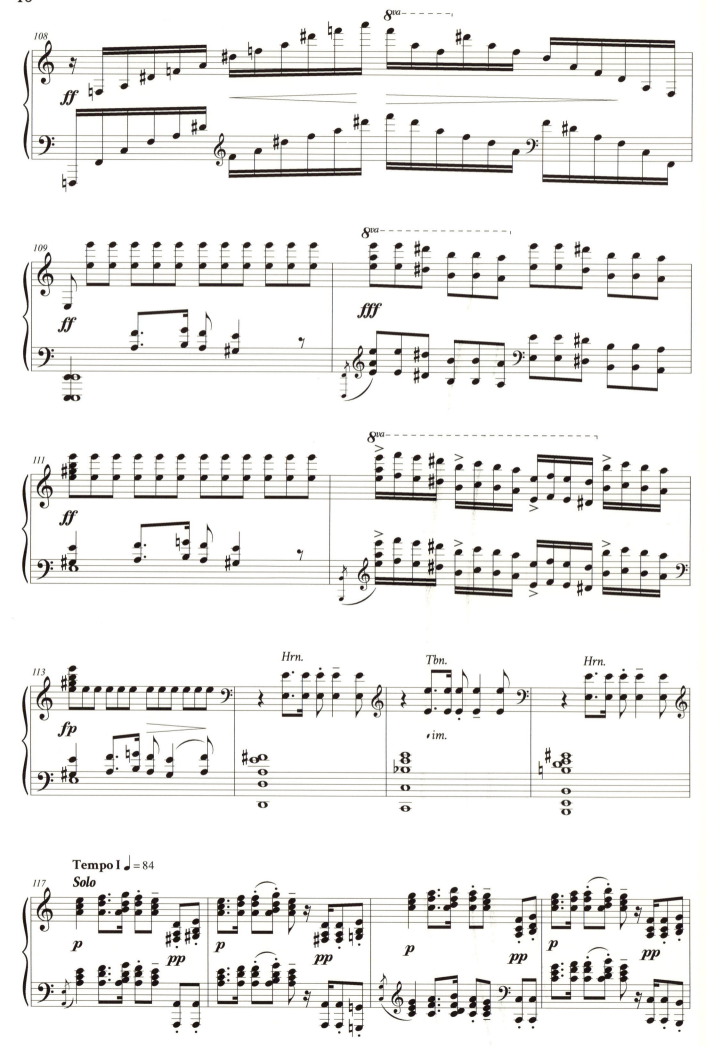

14

16

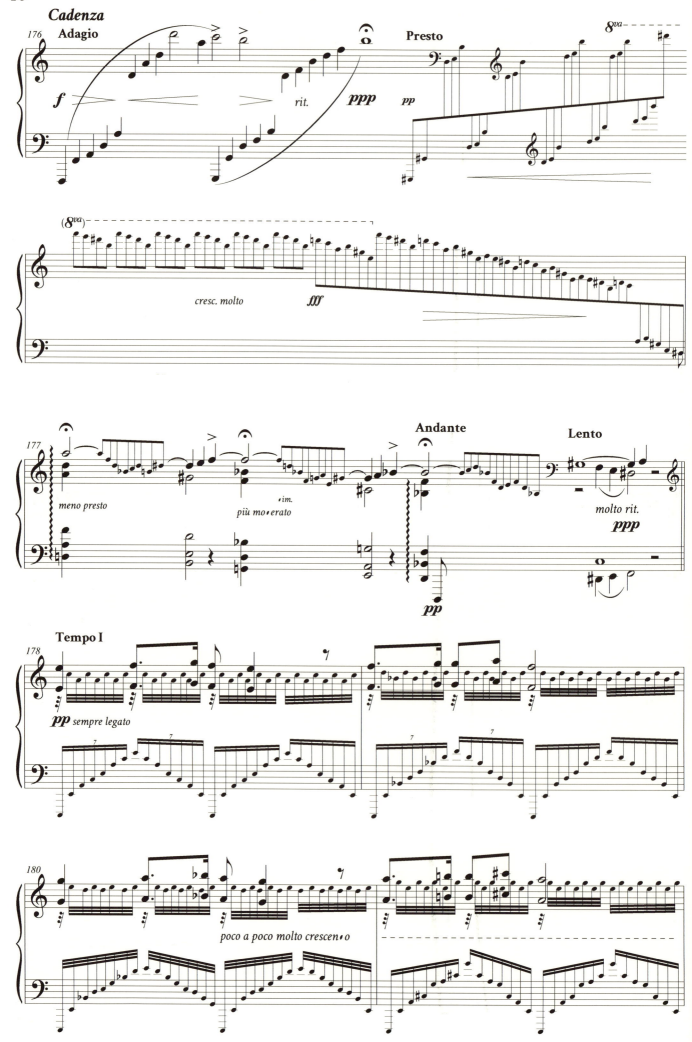

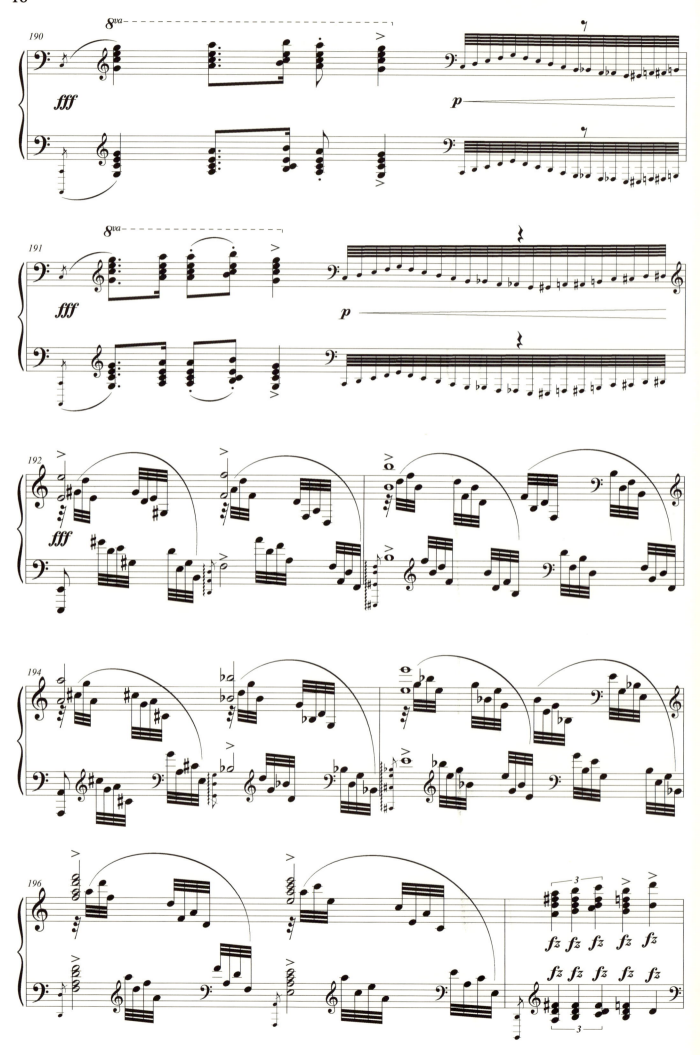

# II

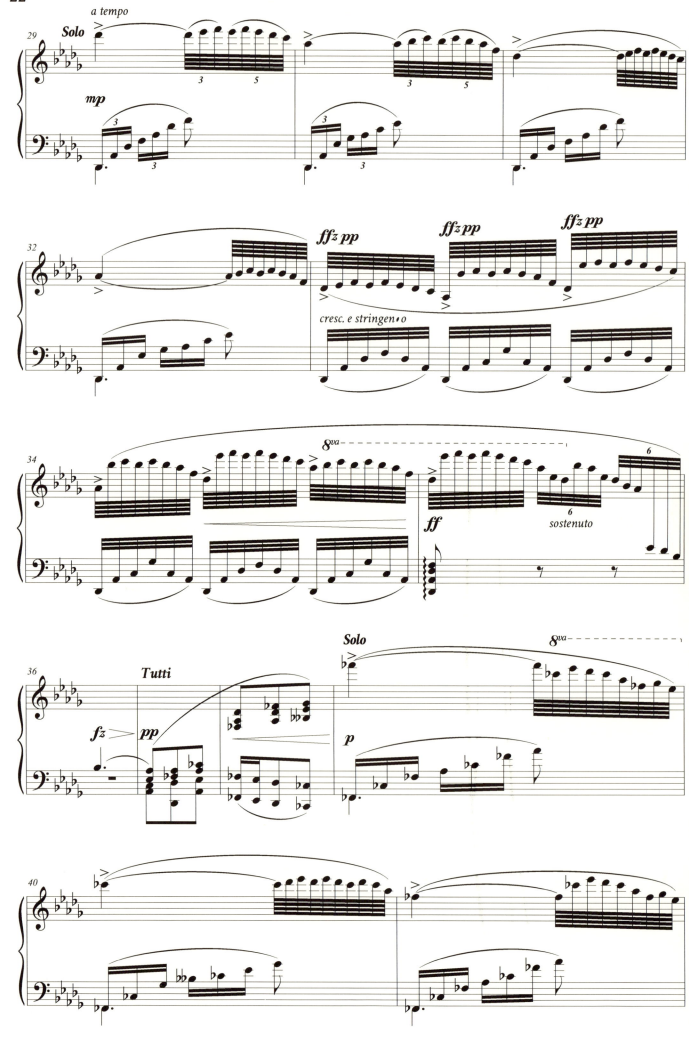

# III

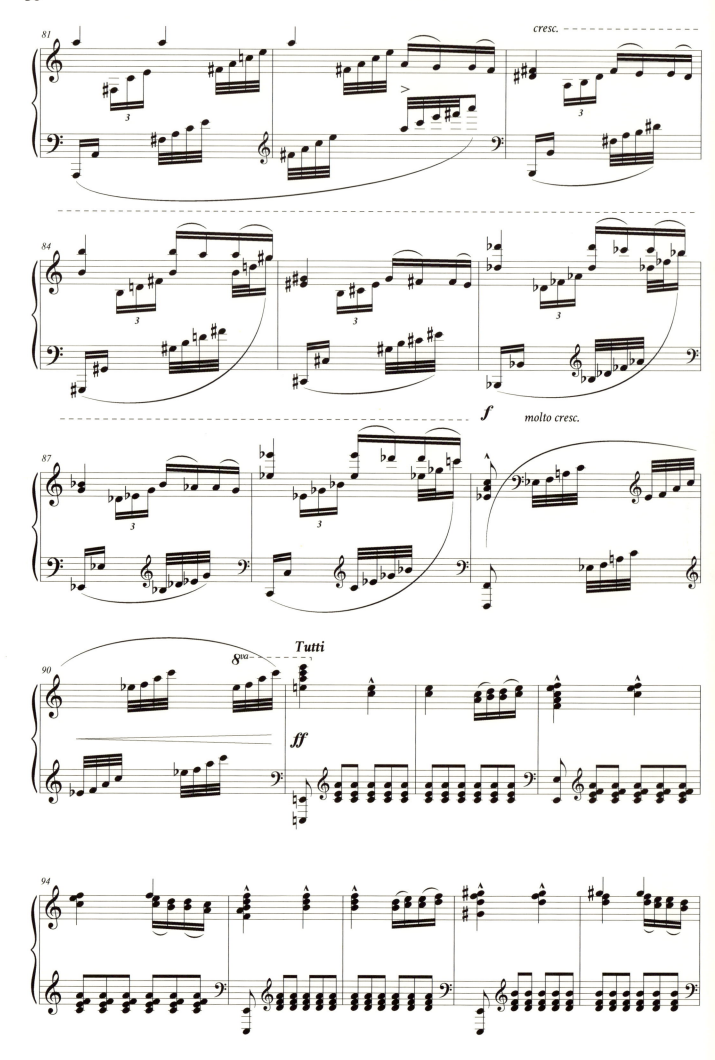

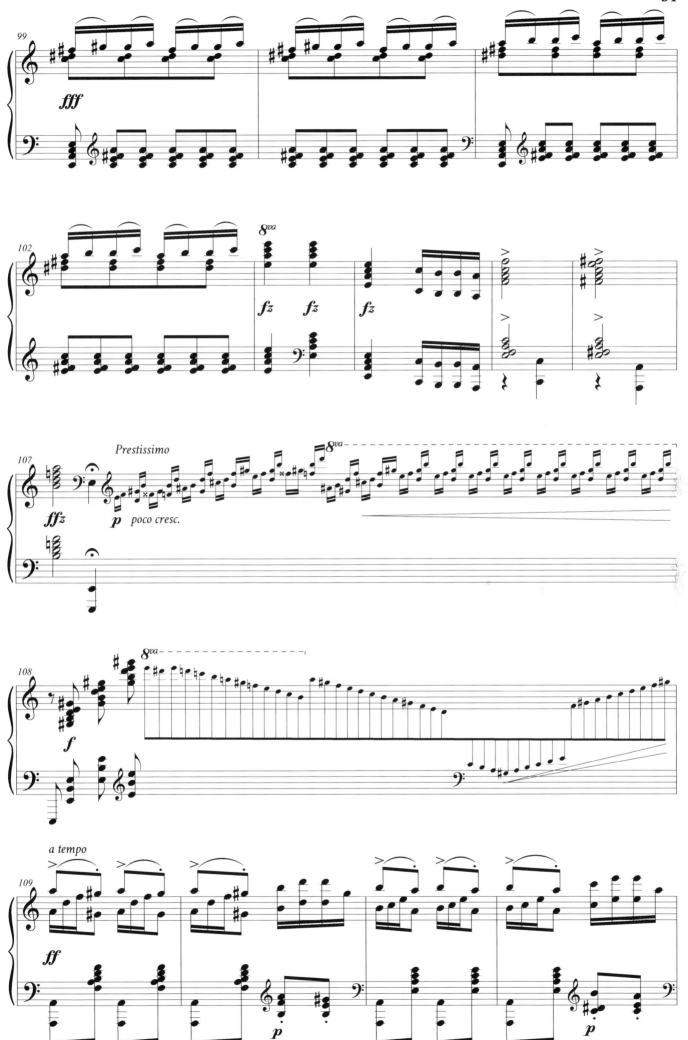

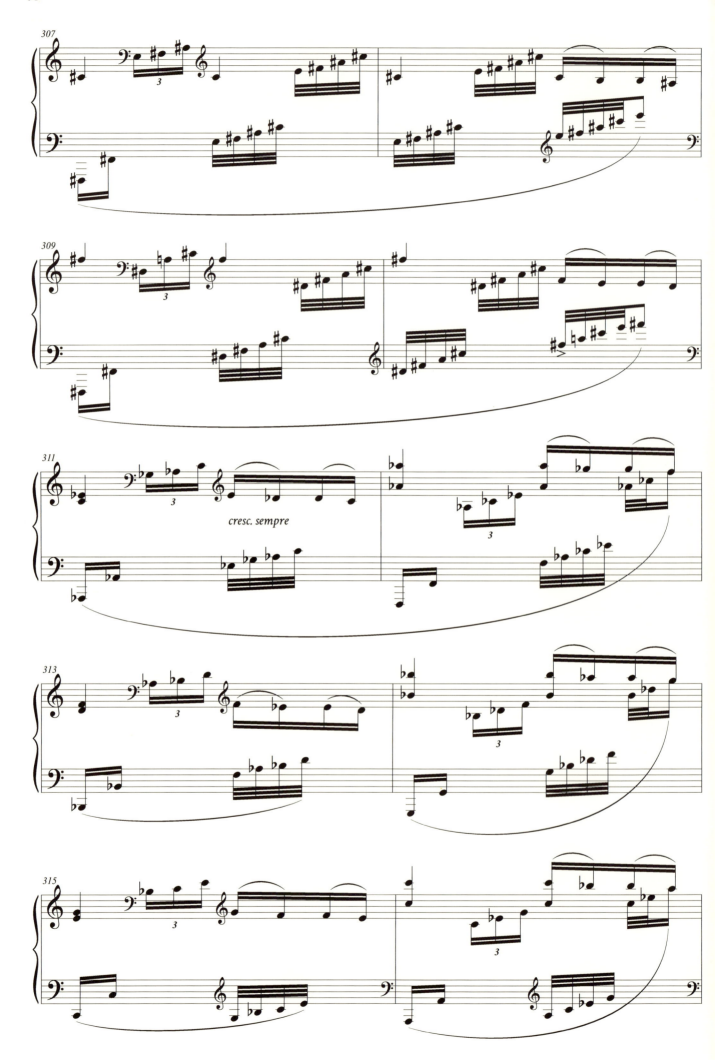

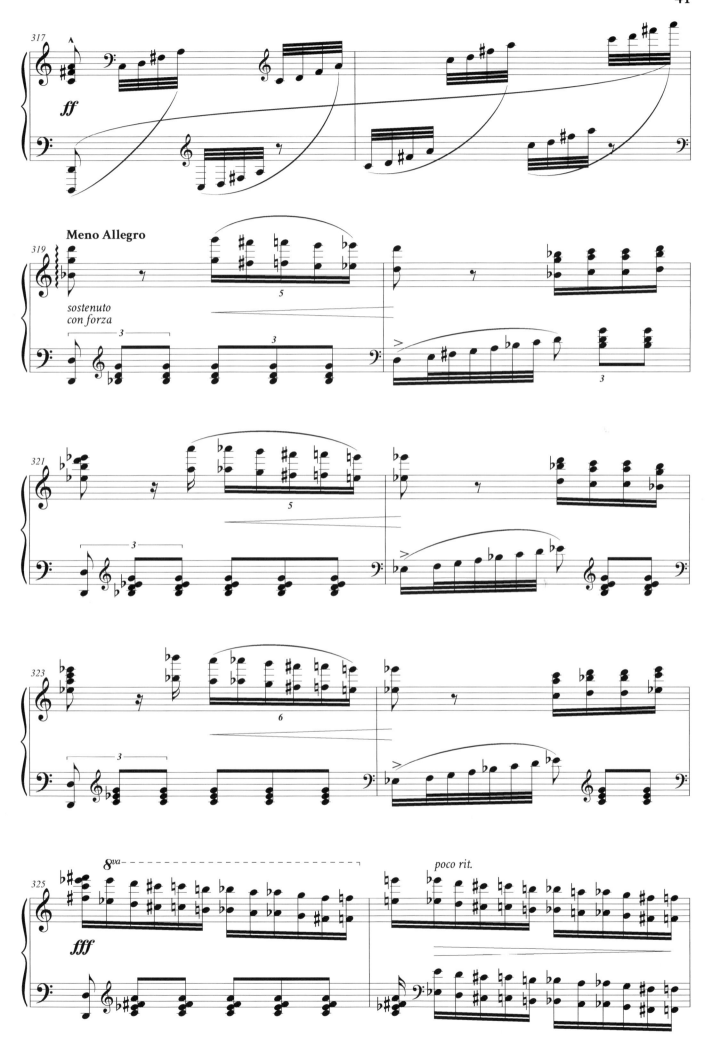

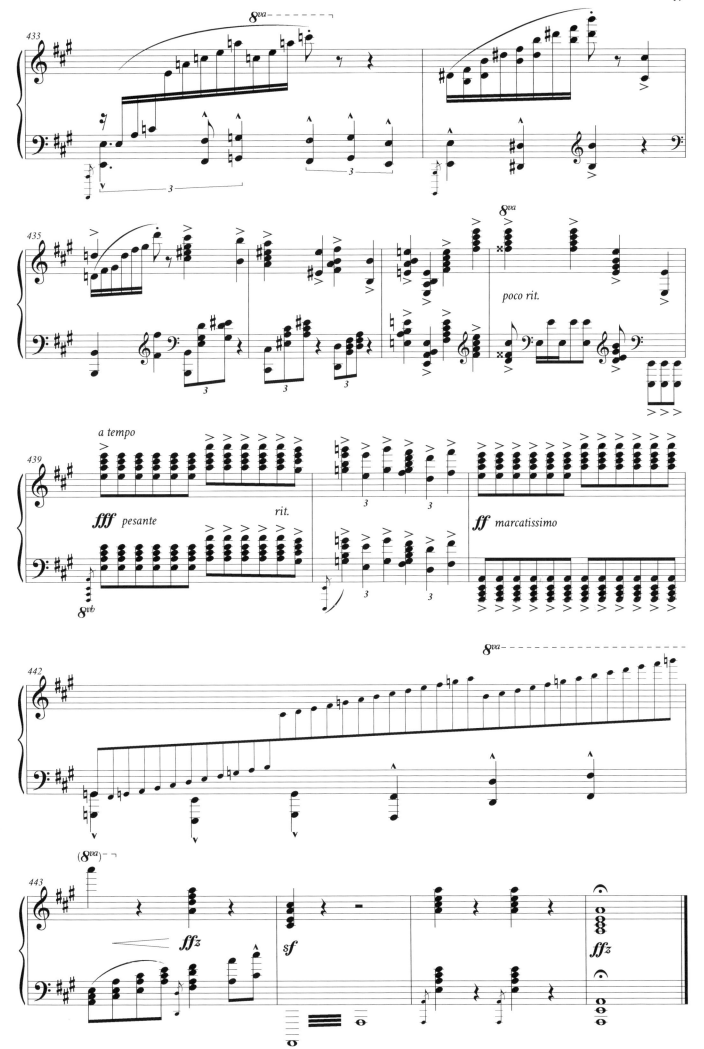

# GRIEG

# Piano Concerto in a minor, Op. 16

# Solo piano arrangement

### MUSICADDICTS EDITION

Composed by Edvard Grieg

Arranged by MusicAddicts

Published by 엠에이기획

1st Printed in May. 14, 2017

Price : 25 USD

ISBN : 9781521232033

출판사 엠에이기획

Tel. +82 32-343-0071

Facebook : @musicaddicts21

Made in the USA
Las Vegas, NV
07 August 2021